Tommy G. Thompson
Governor

Joe Leean
Secretary

State of Wisconsin

Department of Health and Family Se...

October 1, 1999

Dear School Counselor:

Wisconsin Division of Supportive Living and the Wraparound Milwaukee Maternal Breast Cancer Project are pleased to provide you with a copy of *Once Upon a Hopeful Night* by Risa Sacks Yaffe. Ms. Yaffe created this book as a tool to help parents discuss with their children a cancer diagnosis in the family and to open lines of communication so that the specific situations of each family can be addressed. *Once Upon a Hopeful Night,* written for children age 5-11, addresses many of the issues - anger, sadness, fear and hope - facing a young child who has a parent with cancer.

A recent article in the Wall Street Journal profiled the impact of a parent's illness on the child and the role school personnel play in addressing issues for the child and the child's peer group. The article stated that age appropriate resources for explaining a parent's illness to a child are limited. It was this need that led Ms. Yaffe to write her book.

The Oncology Nursing Press reports that the book prepares children for what to expect related to treatment, dispels child misperceptions (e.g. cancer is contagious), and offers reassurance that the child will be loved and cared for despite the parent's illness. The book has been used in hospitals and treatment centers. One oncology social worker writes *"Once Upon a Hopeful Night* is a helpful companion for any parent who has cancer or for their partner in helping to explain the initial diagnosis and treatment and feelings which accompany this illness."

The Milwaukee, Wisconsin Program is part of the Comprehensive Community Mental Health Services for Children and Their Families Program within the Child, Adolescent and Family Branch of the federal Center for Mental Health Services. The Center for Mental Health Services, part of the Substance Abuse and Mental Health Administration, provides national leadership and funding to improve the quality, accessibility, and range of treatment and support services for all Americans with mental health problems and their families. It also supports innovative programs and communicates important information about them to care providers, administrators, consumers, family members, practitioners, and policymakers nationwide. Information about the Center for Mental Health Services and the Comprehensive Community Mental Health Services for Children and Their Families Program is available by calling the National Mental Health Services Knowledge Exchange Network at 1-880-789-2647.

Please accept this copy of *Once Upon a Hopeful Night* as a resource for working with children whose parents have cancer. We encourage you to share the book with other staff; and hope that parents and/or counselors and children read the book together and that counselors be available to provide support and appropriate referrals. Ms. Yaffe has indicated that she would be willing to answer questions or provide any other help you request about talking with children; she can be reached at (301) 251-8521. We appreciate your hard work and look forward to your comments and questions.

Sincerely,

Sinikka McCabe
Administrator

Risa Sacks Yaffe
Author,
Once Upon a Hopeful Night

cc. School Principal

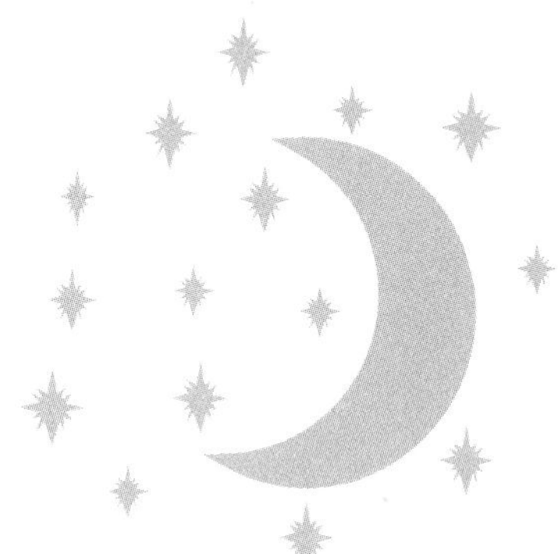

Once Upon a Hopeful Night

by

Risa Sacks Yaffe

Illustrations by Troy Cramer

Oncology Nursing Press, Inc.
A Subsidiary of the Oncology Nursing Society
Pittsburgh, PA

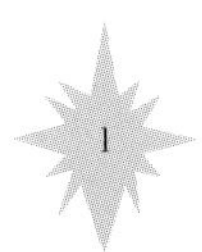

Oncology Nursing Press, Inc.
Technical Publications Editor:
Barbara Sigler, RN, MNEd, CORLN
Staff Editor:
Lisa George, BA
Creative Services Associate:
James Morton

Library of Congress Catalog Card Number: 98-68238

ISBN 1-890504-10-6

Printed in the United States of America.

Oncology Nursing Press, Inc.
A Subsidiary of the Oncology Nursing Society

Dedication

"He who saves one life saves an entire world."

The Talmud

With love and appreciation . . .

For Eric, Dara, and Ethan and all those who saved my world.

Foreword

Many years ago, when some people became mysteriously ill and died, there was no name for what was happening to them. Years later, the illness was identified as cancer. Though doctors knew what it was, they did not know how to cure it, and people continued to die. Ignorance and fear made people feel uncomfortable talking about cancer, while the patient felt isolated from family and friends. As science advanced, treatments were developed that successfully fought and sometimes cured cancer. Although we have advanced medically in the treatment of cancer, we have not advanced psychologically in our ability to talk about it.

Once Upon a Hopeful Night was created as a tool that parents can use to break the news to their children and open the lines of communication so that the specific situations of each family can be addressed. I want parents and children to know that with every day, there is hope for new treatments, hope for recovery, and hope for cure.

Risa Sacks Yaffe

Come sit with me and talk a while, as we so often do,
I have something important that I'd like to share with you.
Though it may be hard to understand what I'm about to say,
In my heart I have to know that you will be okay.

Sometimes when you're feeling sick and can't go out to play,
I keep you home to rest until the illness goes away.
Mommy calls the doctor to tell him what is wrong,
He tells me I should bring you there if you are sick too long.

Moms and dads can get sick, too, and not know what is wrong.
We do the same things children do until we're feeling strong.
The past few weeks I've noticed that I haven't felt my best,
So I went to see our doctor so that he could do some tests.

TROY

Today I've learned the reason why I have felt so bad.
The words he said were scary and made me feel quite sad.
He told me I have cancer. It shocked me . . . made me cry,
Often times as you may hear, it's made some people die.

TROY

But keep in mind that many live. That's what I plan to do;
To stay around for years to come and take good care of you.
We found the illness early that is making me so sick,
A treatment's most successful when you start it really quick.

TROY

It's nothing that we said or did that made the cancer come,
The doctors really are unsure of where it does come from.
There is so much that is unknown, sometimes it's hard to cope,
But even if we're mad or sad, we'll never give up hope.

TROY

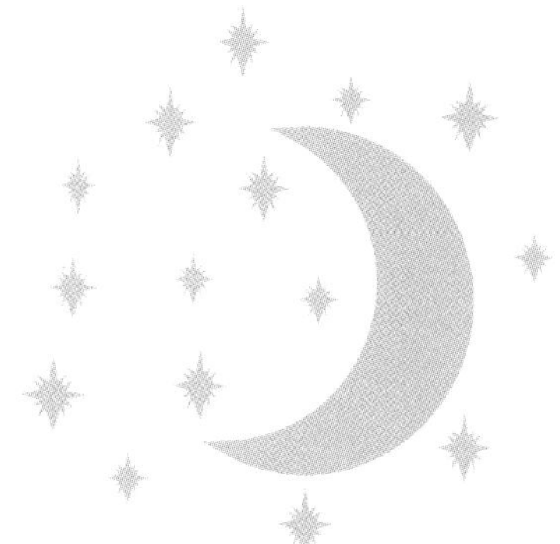

We'll do the things we like to do the same as we do now,
Should I become unable, we'll find some way somehow.
We'll pass our days the usual ways, you'll go to school and play,
I'll help you with your homework and read you stories every day.

TROY

Sometimes things may be hectic; you won't know what to do,
But you should know that always, someone's here
to care for you.
Our friends will come, and family, too,
to help us fight this fight,
And you can talk to all of us about your fears and fright.

Hospitals and waiting rooms are places I'll have to be,
To get the kind of care the doctors say is best for me.
I may not have to stay there, but if by chance I do,
Then you can call me on the phone and even visit, too.

TROY

The medicine they'll give me is chemotherapy,
It's very strong and helps to fight this illness we can't see.
It fights the cancer very hard, and it can cause a scare,
The way my body may react is by losing weight and hair.

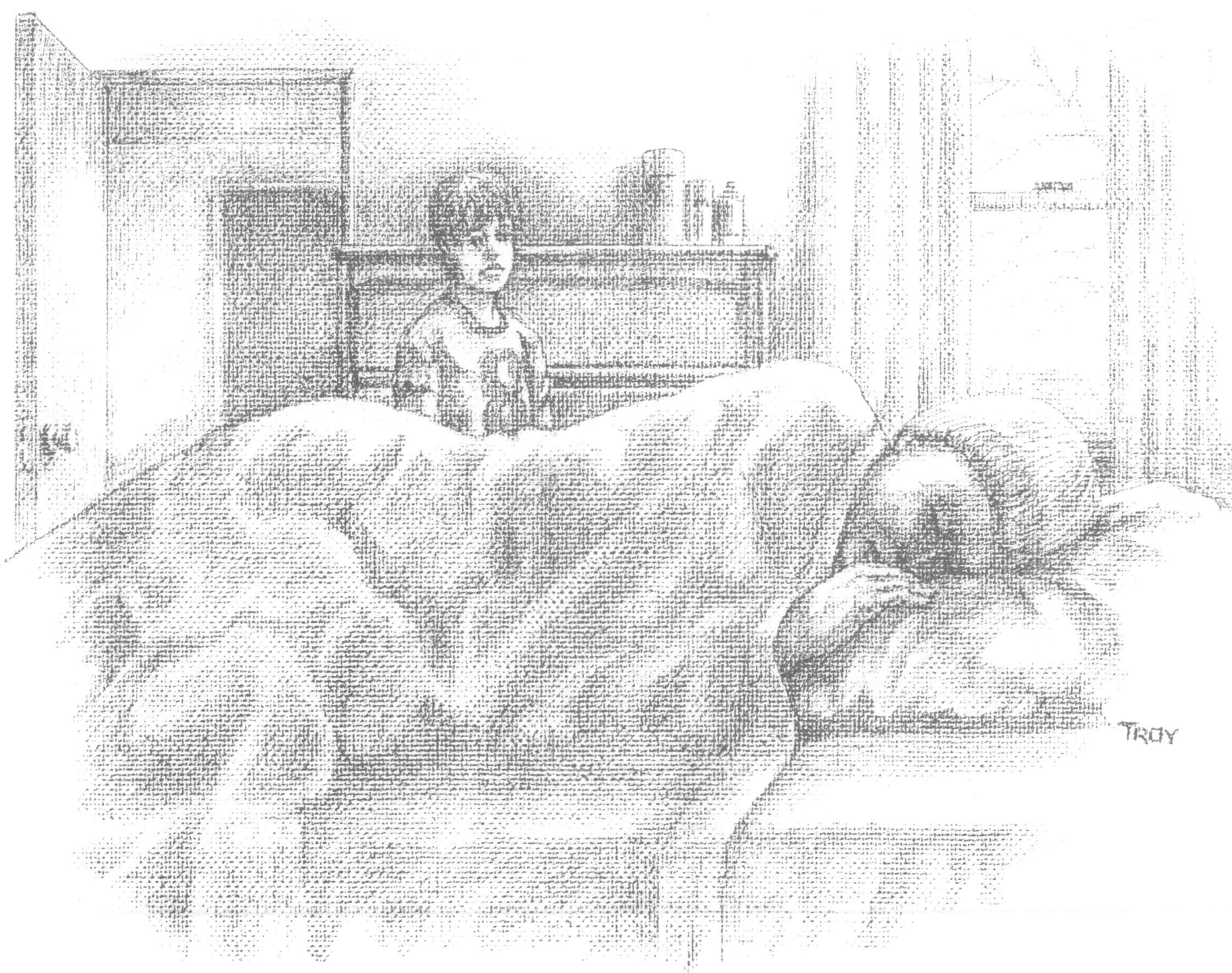
TROY

Some days I may be very sick or tired and need rest,
But other days I might be fine and feeling at my best.
My body will be fighting with all its energy,
To get rid of this cancer that's now a part of me.

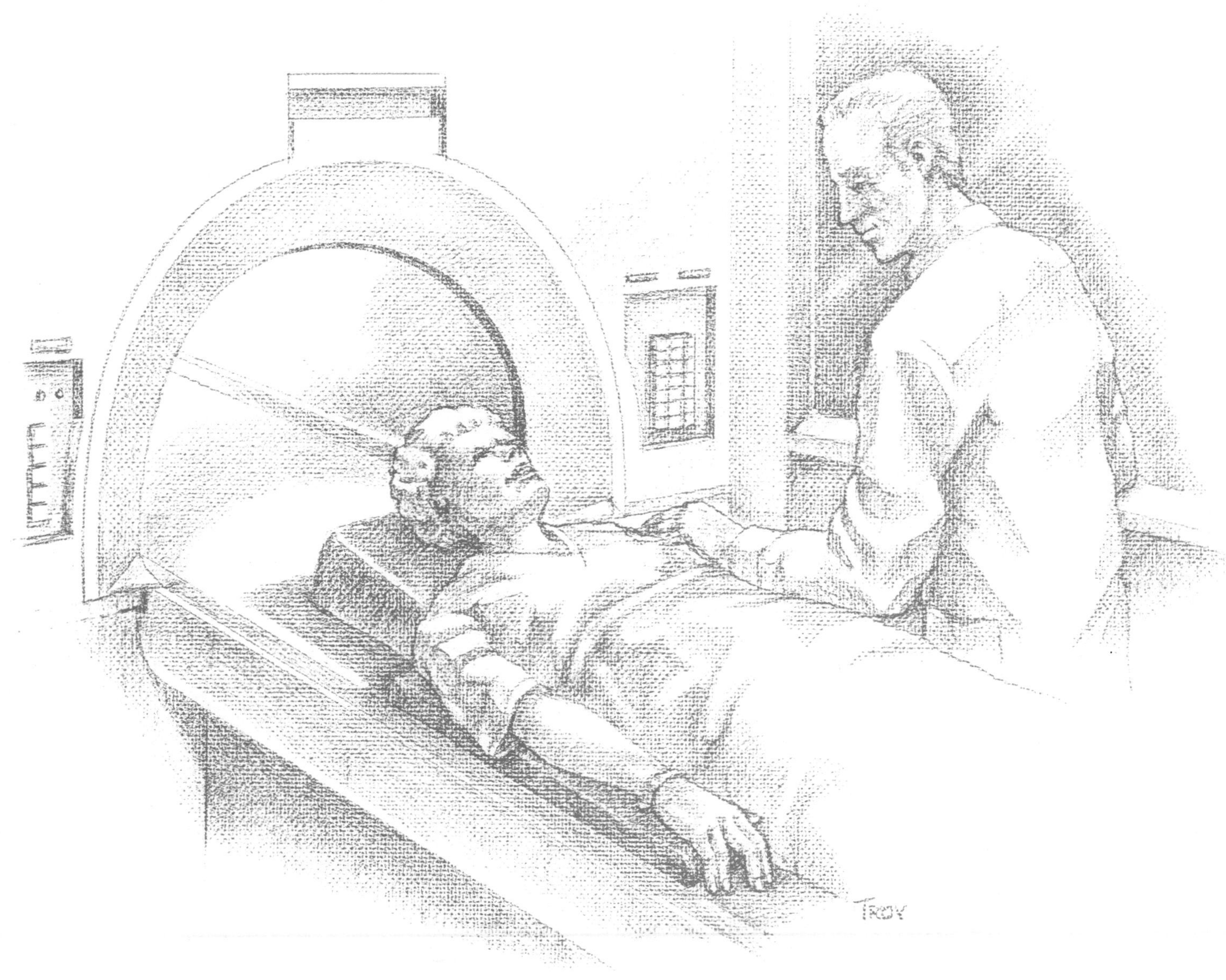
TROY

Doctors will do tests to see if I am getting well.
X-rays, scans, and blood tests are the things they use to tell.
They do them without any pain and finish in a hurry,
And let us know what's happening so we won't sit and worry.

TROY

Now if you think that you can't help to make me well and strong,
Then let me tell you right away that you are very wrong.
A laugh, a smile and hug from you can turn a dark day light,
The happiness you bring me can make the wrong seem right.

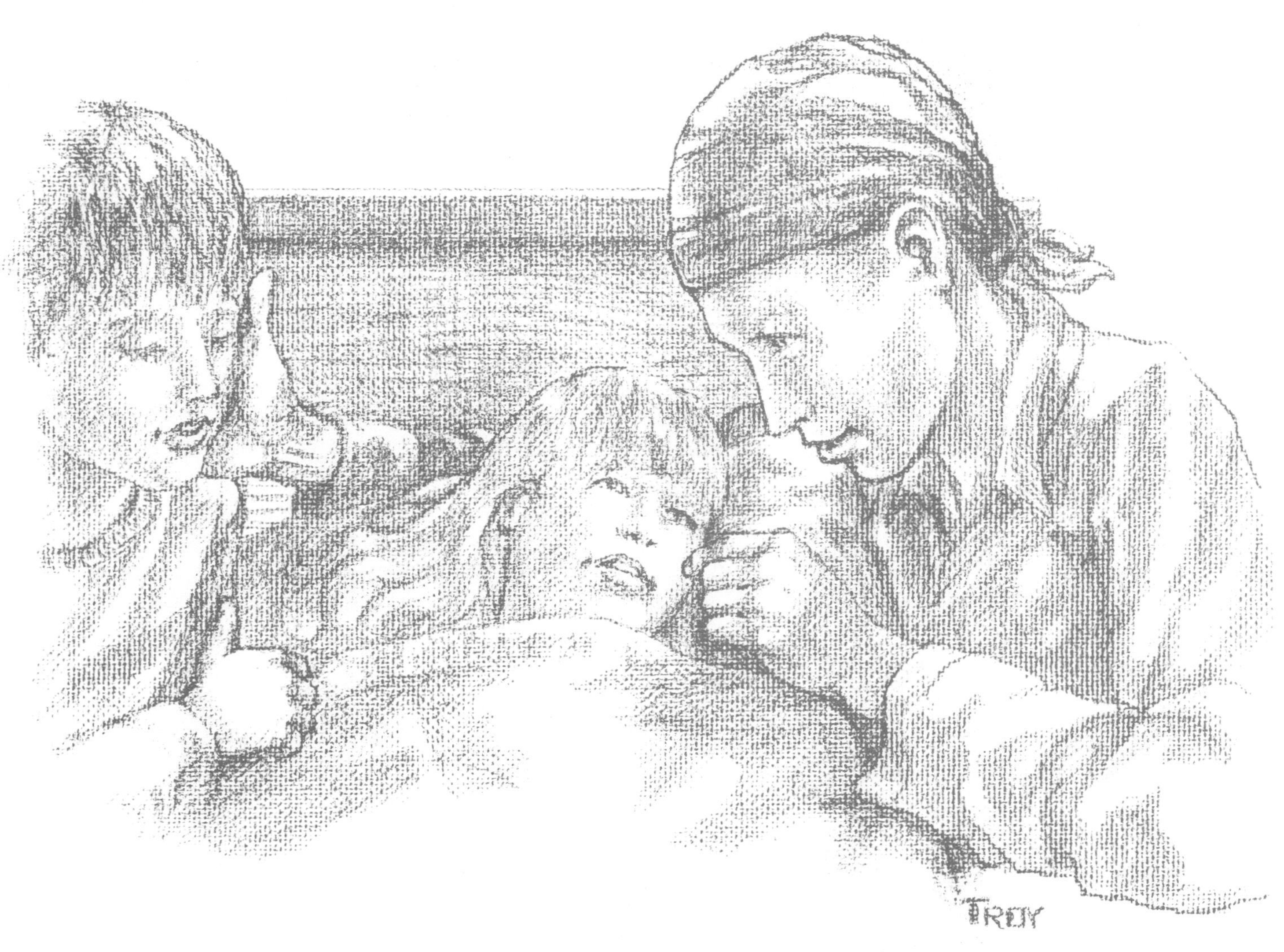
TROY

Once upon a hopeful night,
a mommy kissed her kids goodnight.
She talked to them to ease their fears,
and held them as she wiped their tears.
She tucked them in and hugged them tight,
Once Upon a Hopeful Night.

About the Oncology Nursing Society

The Oncology Nursing Society (ONS) is a national organization of more than 27,000 registered nurses and other healthcare professionals dedicated to excellence in patient care, teaching, research, administration, and education in the field of oncology.

The mission of ONS is to promote excellence in oncology nursing and quality cancer care. The Society works to fulfill this mission by providing nurses and healthcare professionals with access to the highest quality educational programs, cancer-care resources, research opportunities, and networks for peer support.

The vision of ONS is to lead the transformation of cancer care. The Society pursues this vision by initiating and actively supporting educational, legislative, and public awareness efforts to improve the care of people with cancer.

About the Oncology Nursing Press, Inc.

The Oncology Nursing Press, Inc., is a subsidiary of the Oncology Nursing Society, publishing the *Oncology Nursing Forum*, *Clinical Journal of Oncology Nursing*, *ONS News*, ONS Online, and a variety of oncology-nursing publications. Recently, the Press has increased its scope to become a full-range publisher, specializing in books and electronic media pertaining to cancer care.

Also available from the Oncology Nursing Press, Inc.

Teenage Cancer Journey
Kathleen Gill

This book addresses the unique issues facing teenagers with cancer, and captures the adolescent's battle with cancer during the transition from child to adult. It describes the author's personal struggles with philosophical questions ("Why me?") and offers advice to teens on losing their hair, relating to friends and family who aren't sick, and balancing school responsibilities while undergoing treatment. The book provides a brief introduction to cancer, and offers advice from others who've battled cancer as teens.

This book is a helpful resource for young people with cancer, as well as for family and friends who want to understand the teenage cancer experience.

Softcover. Approx. 200 pages. Illustrations. 1999.
Price–$18

Stevie's New Blood
Kathryn Ulberg Lilleby

This book tells the story of Stevie who is having a bone marrow transplant in hopes that his leukemia will be cured. Anna, his sister, is his donor and will learn what it is like to give her bone marrow. Stevie's New Blood describes what a bone marrow transplant is like from a child's point of view. It can be adapted for children of various ages. The pictures will tell the story for younger children who cannot read; a 6–10 year old child will be able to read the easy words in large print; and the smaller print on the opposing page will give more detailed information for older readers and parents. It can also be adapted for the child whose parent is having a transplant or for the friend of a child having a bone marrow transplant.

Softcover. Illustrations. 2000
For information on pricing, please contact the Oncology Nursing Press, Inc.

To order copies of books published by the Oncology Nursing Press, Inc. please use the order form on the reverse or contact the Oncology Nursing Press at 412-921-7373.
E-mail: customer.service@ons.org

Oncology Nursing Press, Inc. Publications Order Form

Once Upon A Hopeful Night–$7

Teenage Cancer Journey–$18

Stevie's New Blood–*For information on pricing, please contact the Oncology Nursing Press, Inc.*

A check (made payable to the Oncology Nursing Press, Inc.) or credit card information must accompany your order.

❒ Check ❒ Visa ❒ Master Card ❒ American Express

Credit Card #____________________ Exp. __________

Name____________________

Address ____________________

City____________________ State______ Zip______

Signature ____________________ Phone __________

Book Title	Qty.	Price	Total
		PA residents must include 7% sales tax.	
		Type of Shipping	
		Shipping Charges	
TEEN		Total	

Allow 2-3 weeks for delivery. Order within the US will be shipped UPS Ground (unless otherwise specified). Orders outside the US will be shipped USPS Express Mail International. Next Day Air Service is available at actual cost (you will be charged/invoiced). If actual shipping cost exceeds amounts shown here, you may be charged the difference.

Shipping and handling charges within the US:

Orders up to $25	$5
$25.01 to $50	$6
$50.01 to $100	$7
More than $100	7% of total purchase price
Outside the US:	40% of total purchase price

The Oncology Nursing Press, Inc. will accept returns and will refund all but 15% of the original cost of the merchandise subject to the following restrictions: the current edition must still be in circulation, the sender will absorb the shipping and postage charges for returns, and no refunds will be made after 60 days from the date shipped.

There is a 10% discount on a purchase of ten or more copies of the same item. Mail your order to:
Oncology Nursing Press, Inc., Department 400295, Pittsburgh, PA 15268-0295 or fax to: 412-921-6565.